TOWERS

VAL SINGLETON

Phased Coloring Book

TOWERS

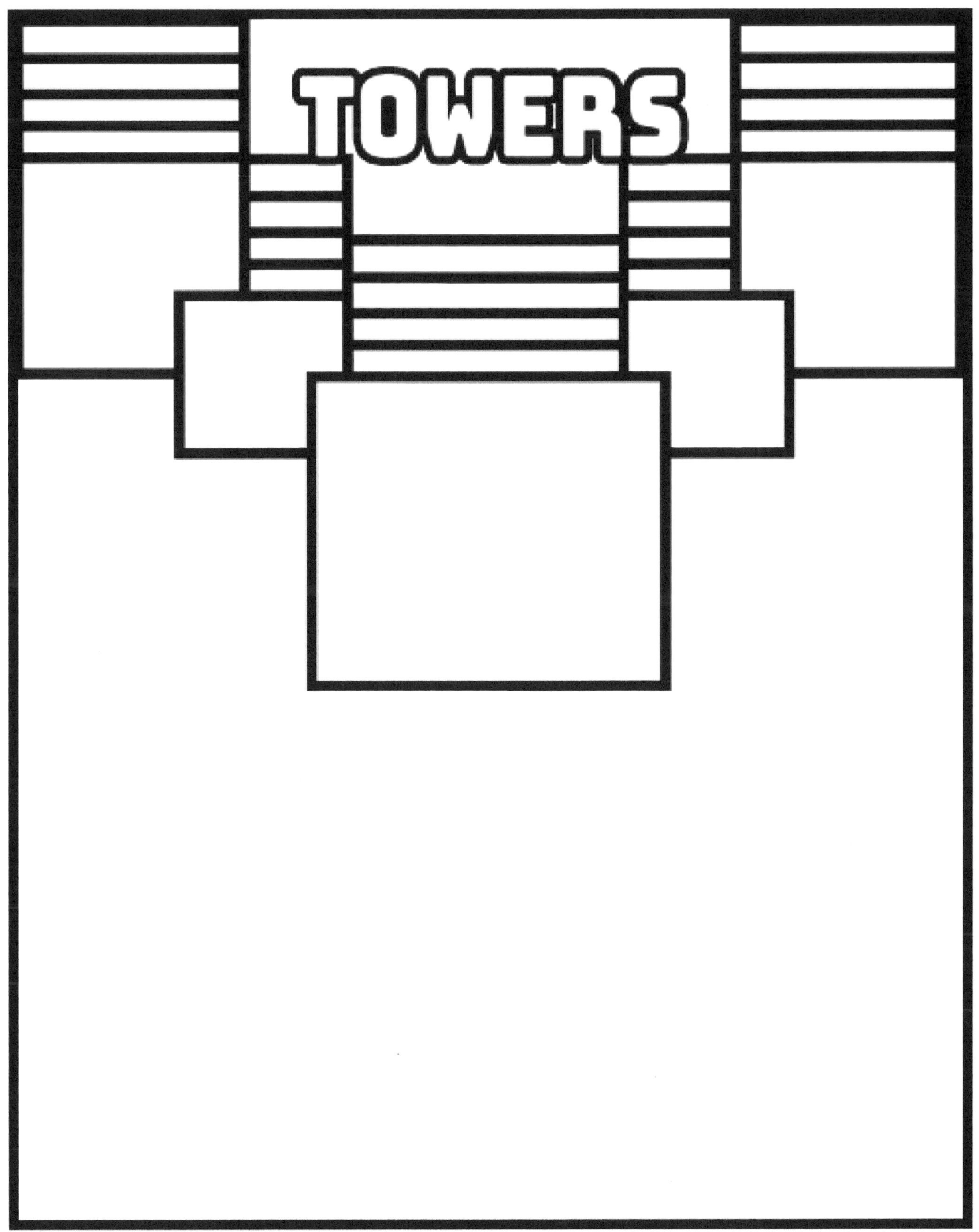

TOWERS

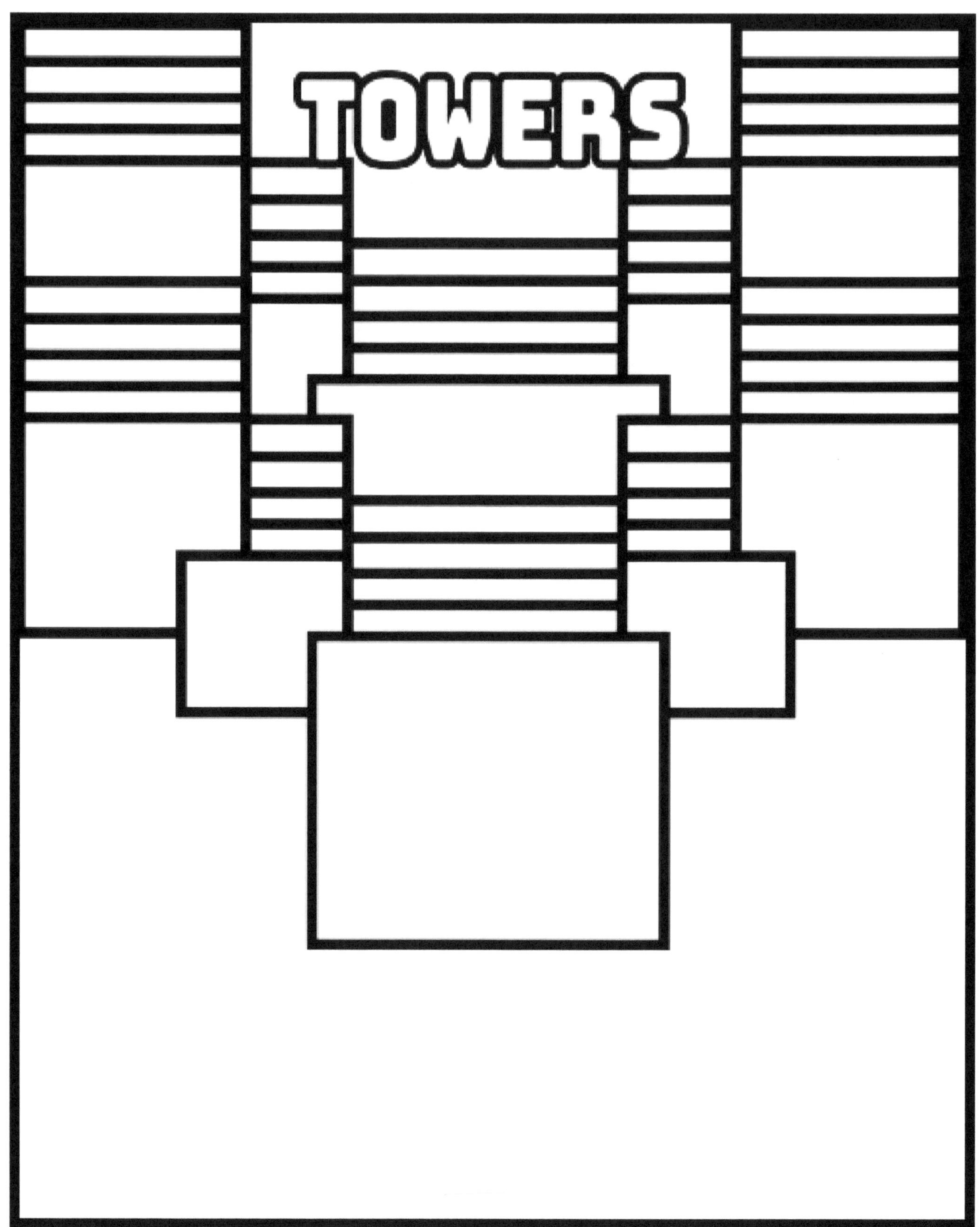
TOWERS

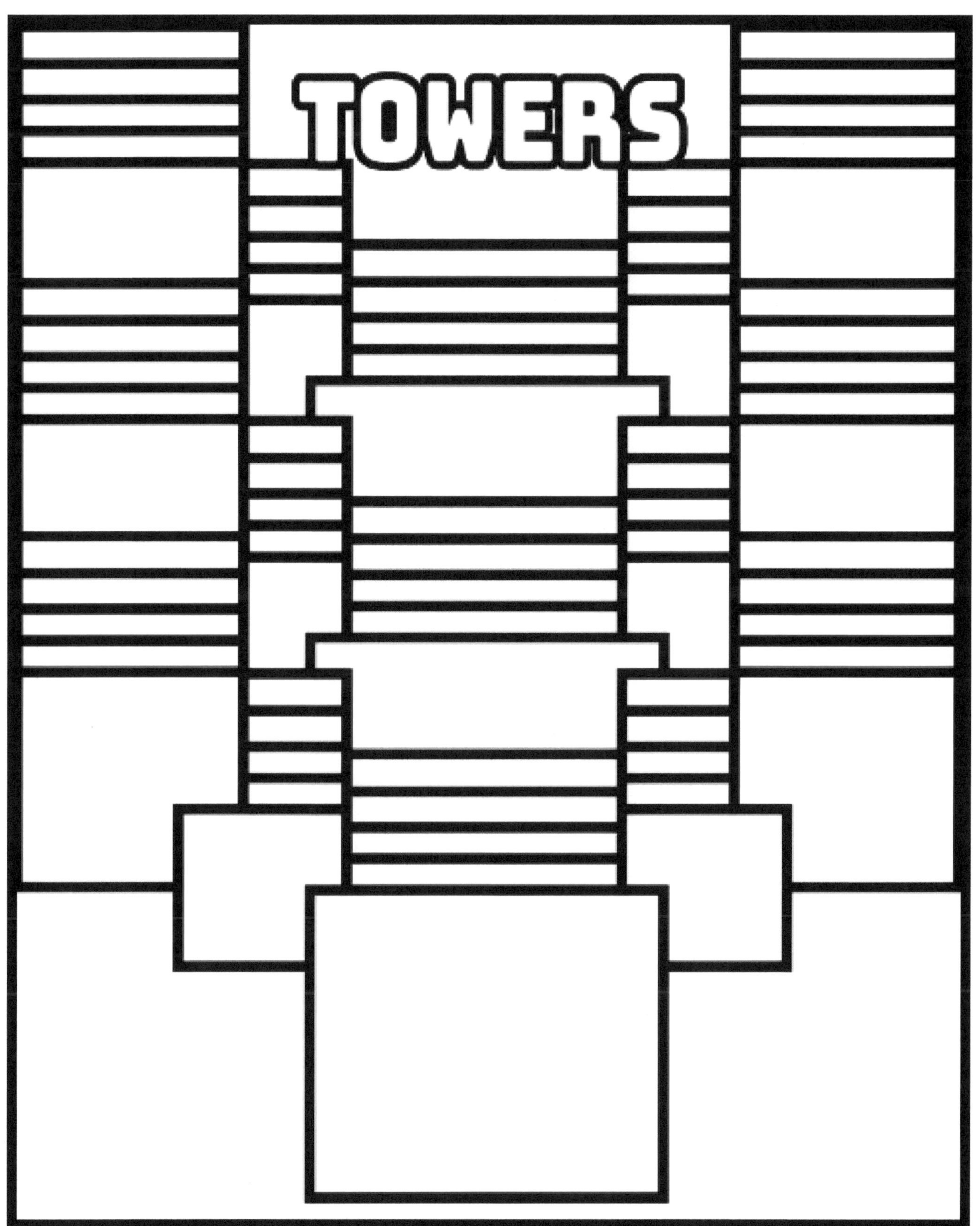

TOWERS

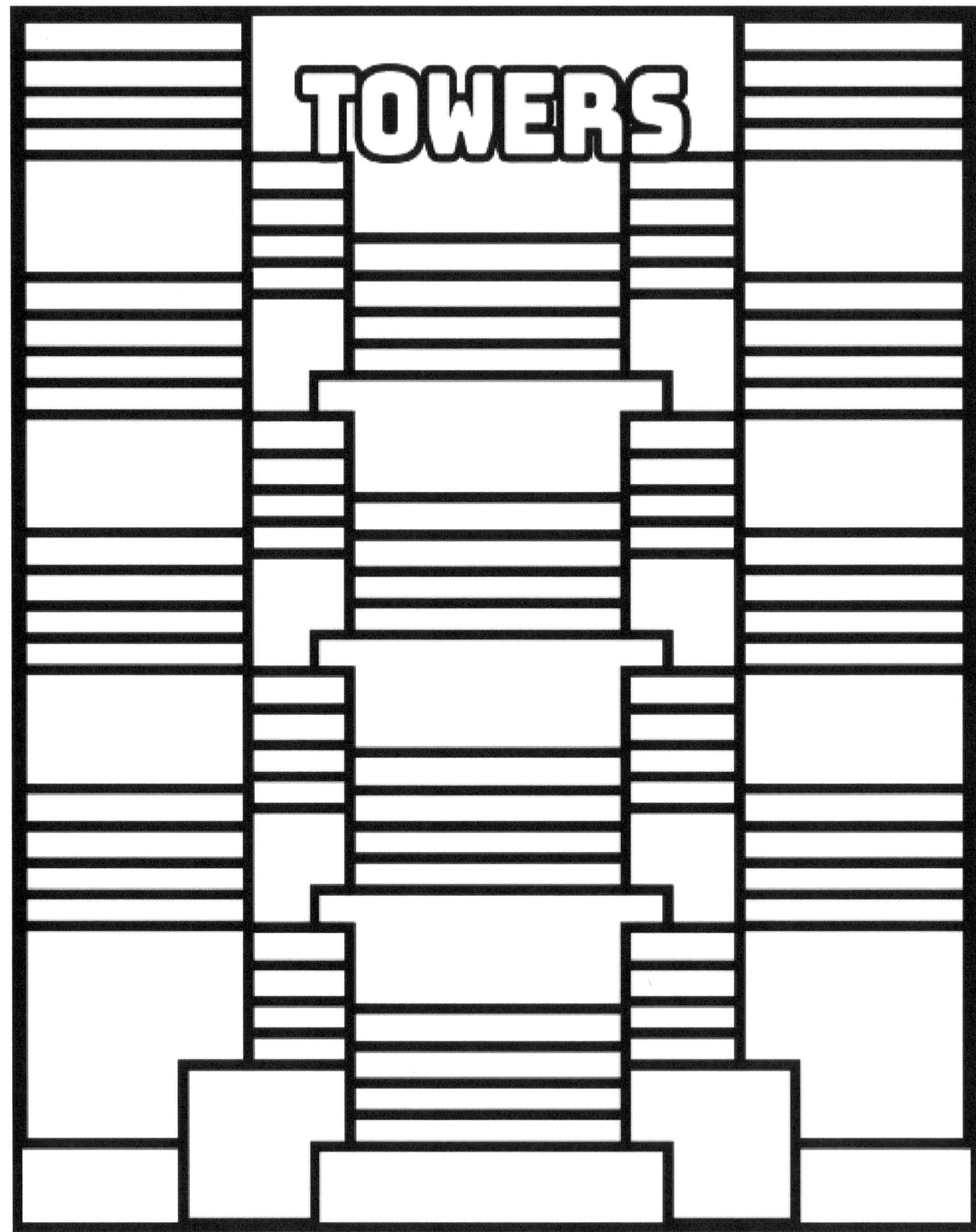
TOWERS

TOWERS

TOWERS

TOWERS

TOWERS

TOWERS

TOWERS

TOWERS

TOWERS

TOWERS

TOWERS

TOWERS

TOWER
TOWER
TOWER
TOWER
TOWER

TOWERS

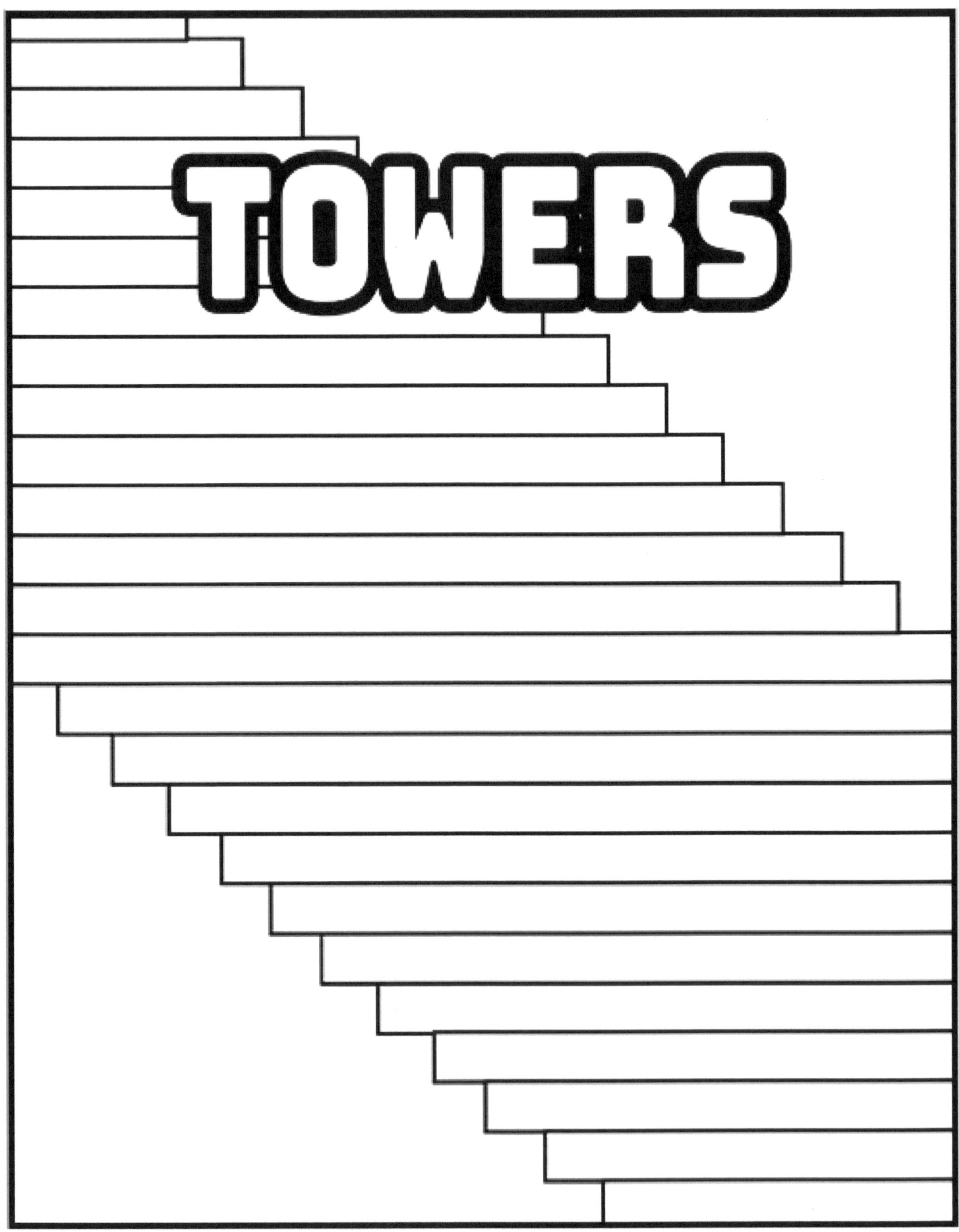

TOWERS

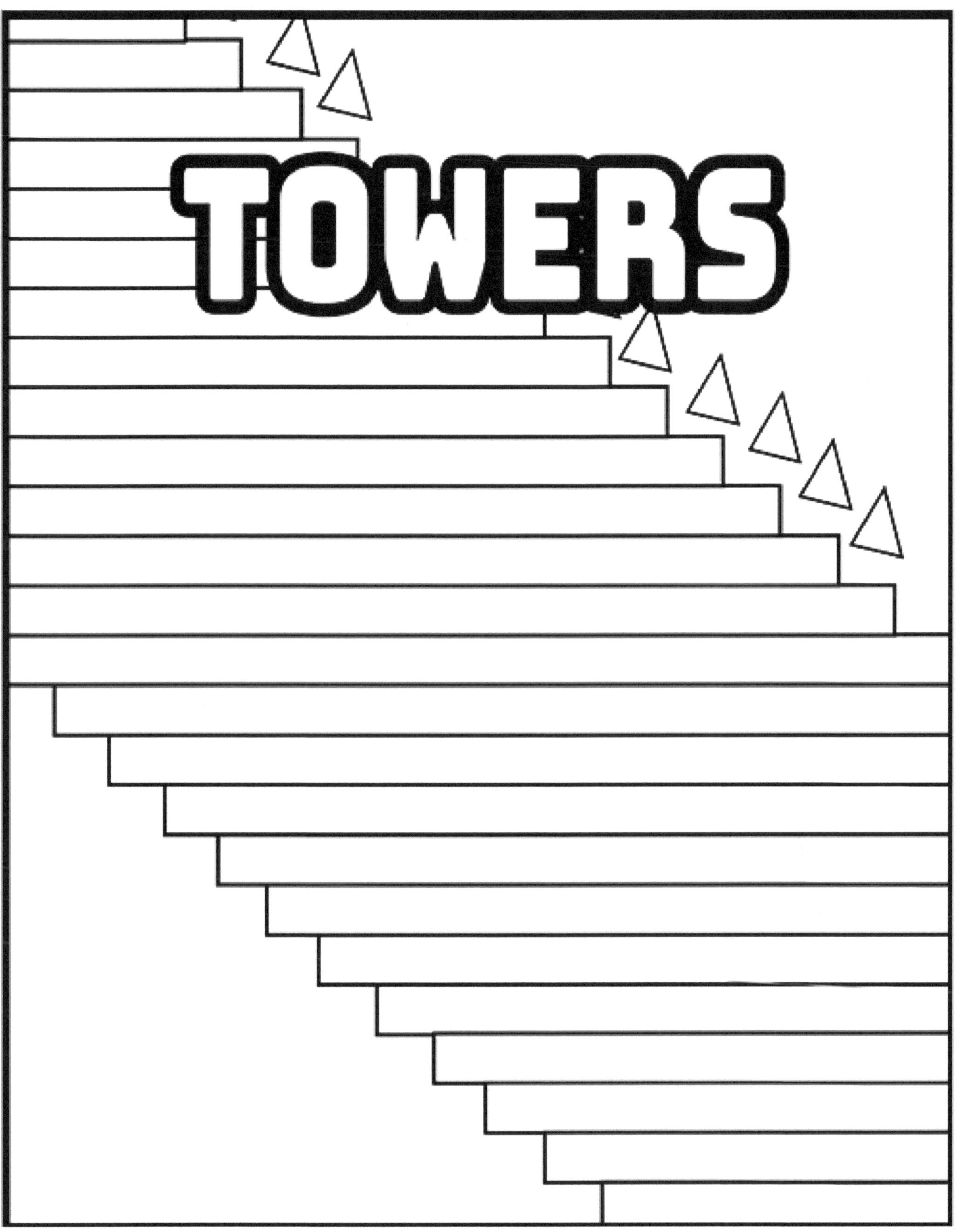

TOWERS

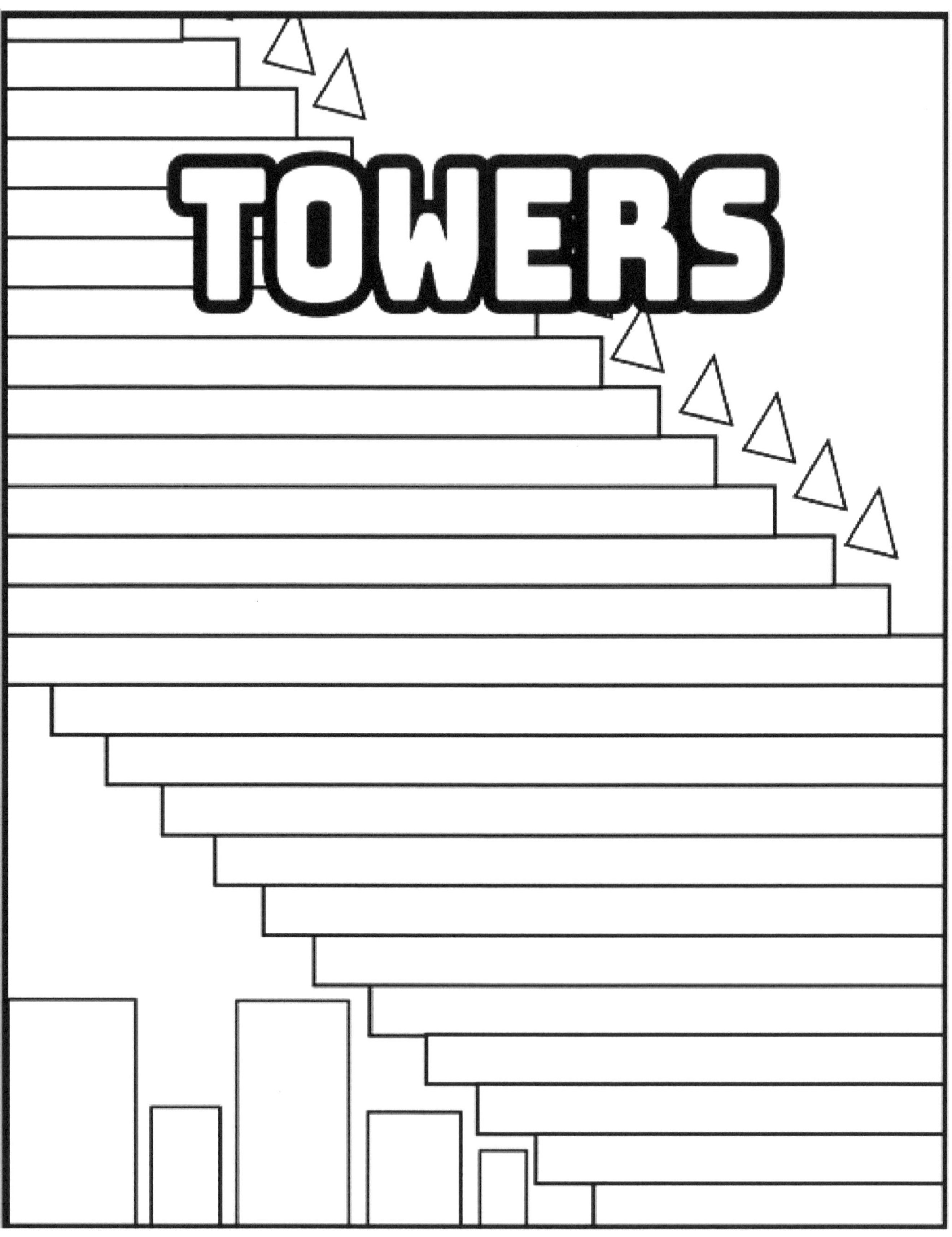

TOWERS

TOWERS

TOWERS

TOWERS

TOWERS

TOWERS

TOWERS

TOWERS

TOWERS

TOWERS

TOWERS

To Reach
or Rise
To a great height

TOWERS

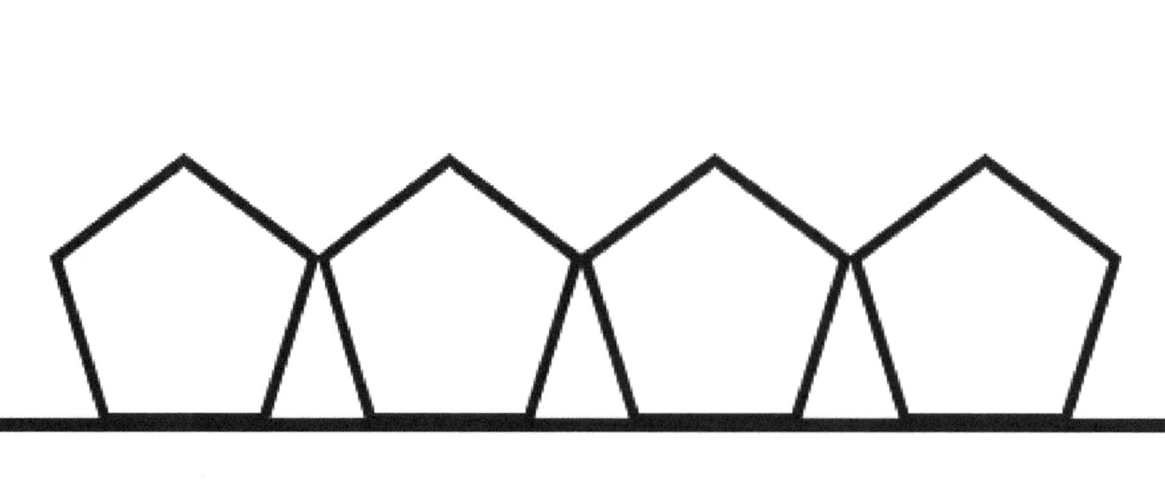

TOWERS

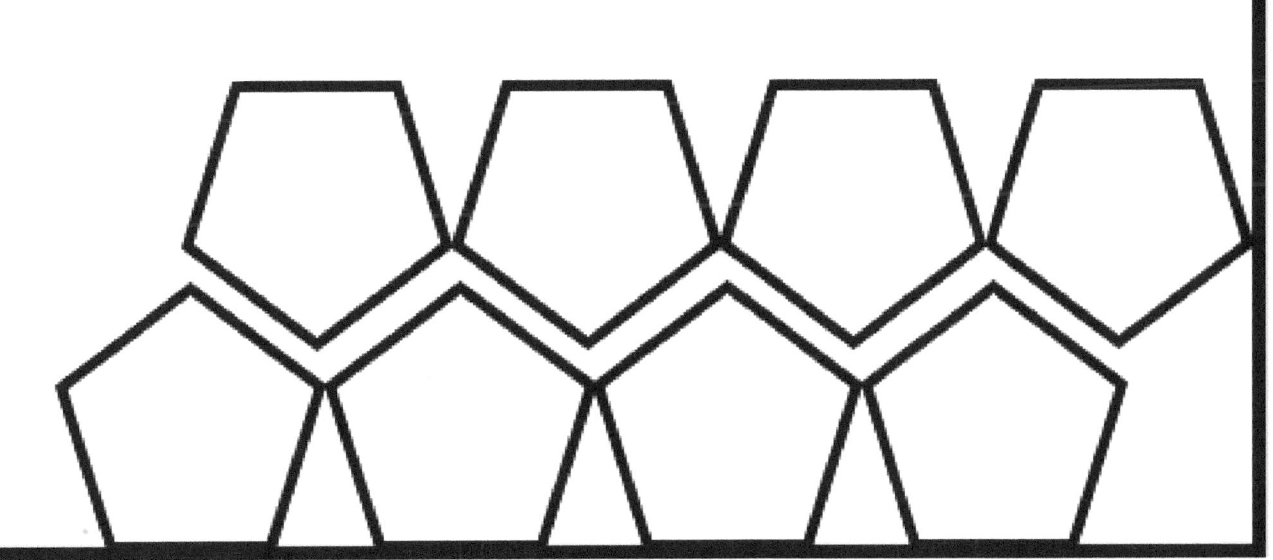

TOWERS

TOWERS

TOWERS

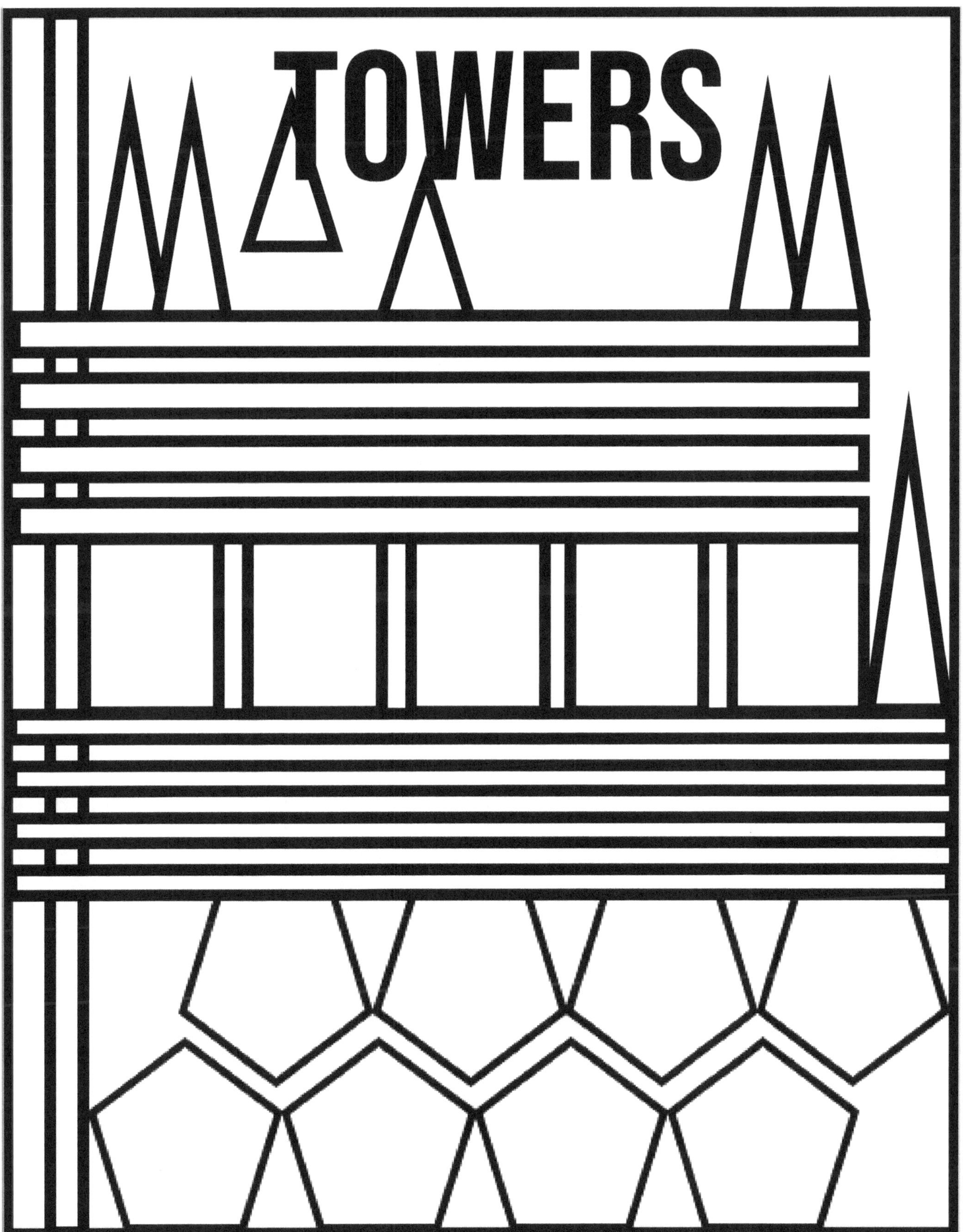
TOWERS

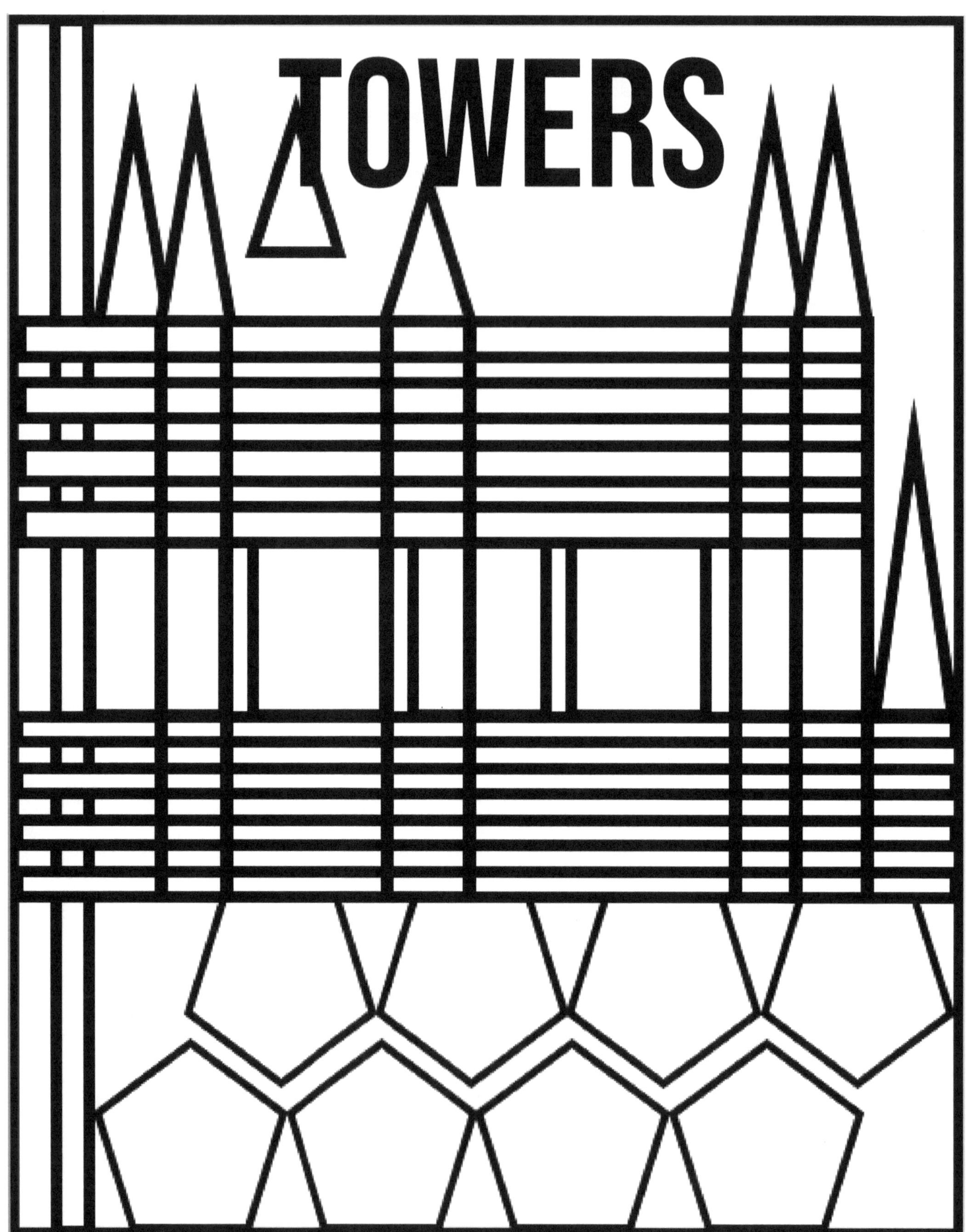
TOWERS

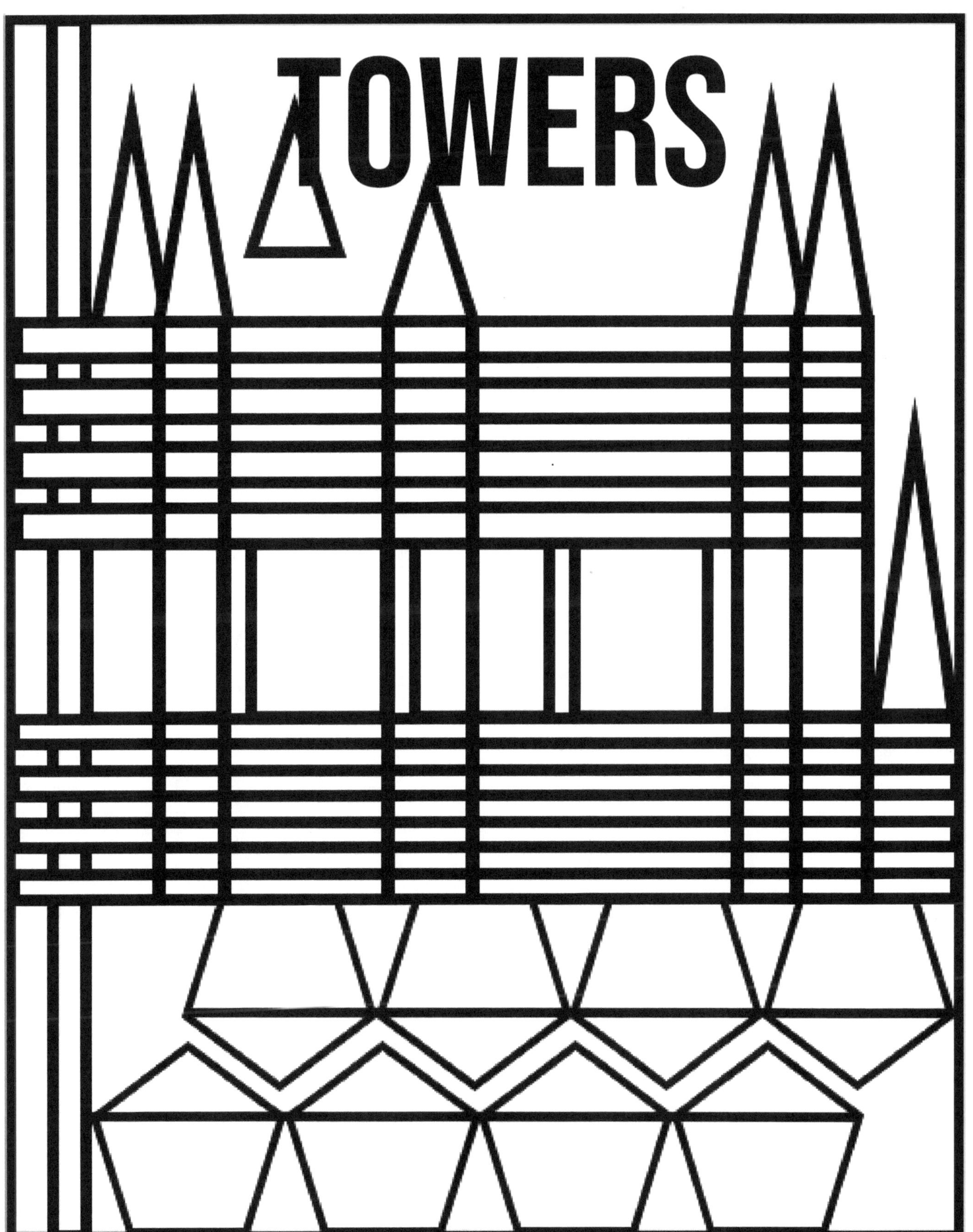
TOWERS

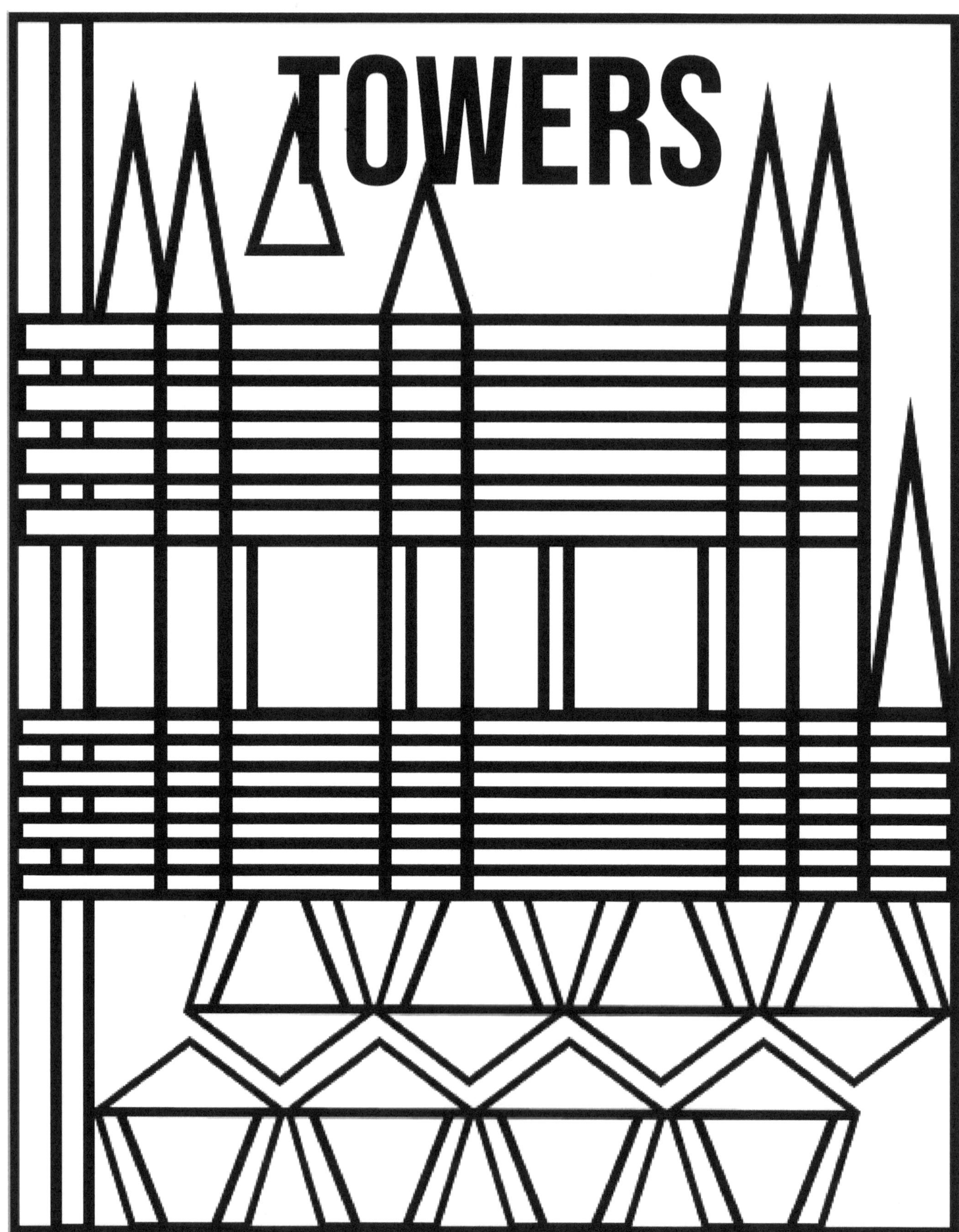
TOWERS

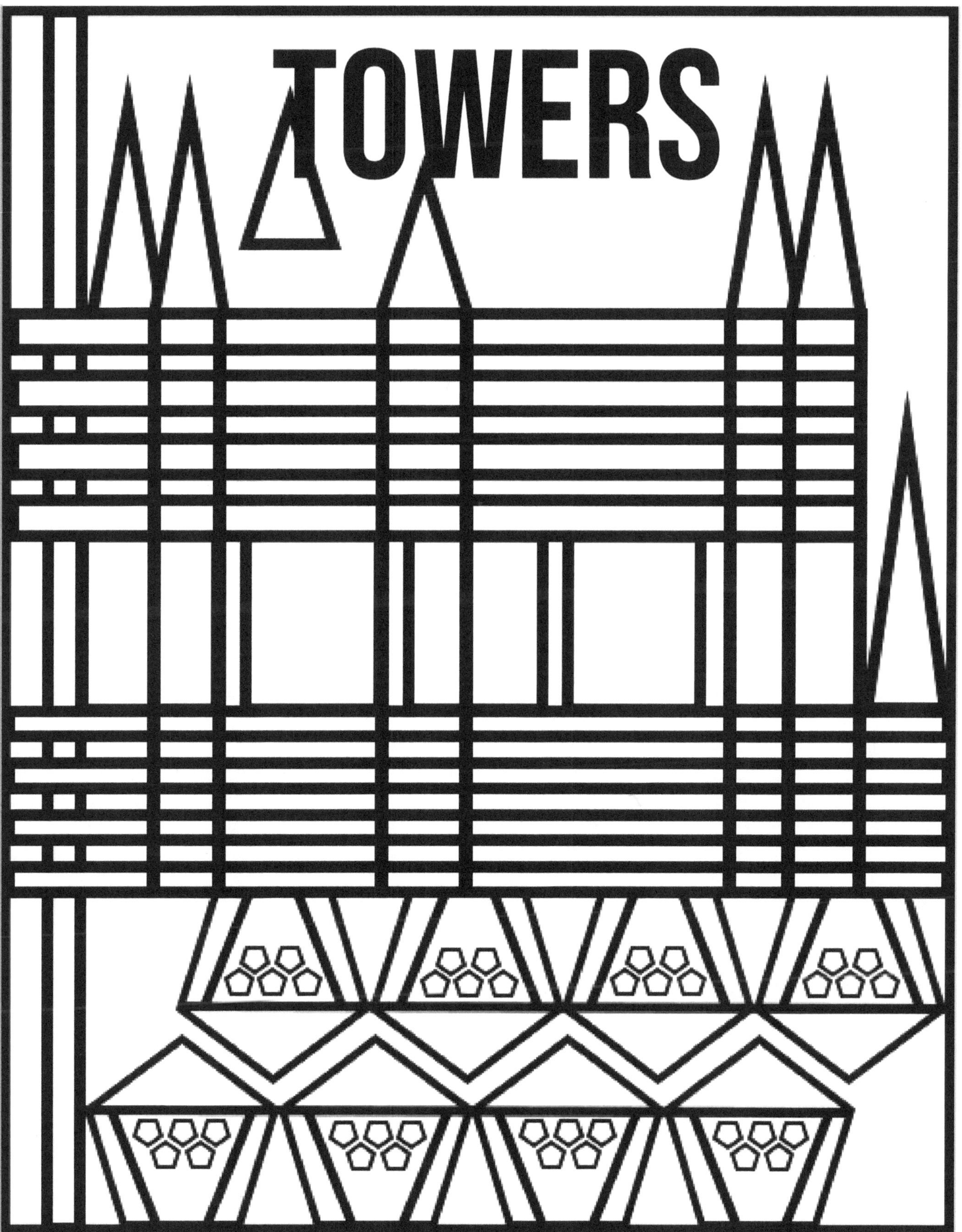
TOWERS

TOWERS

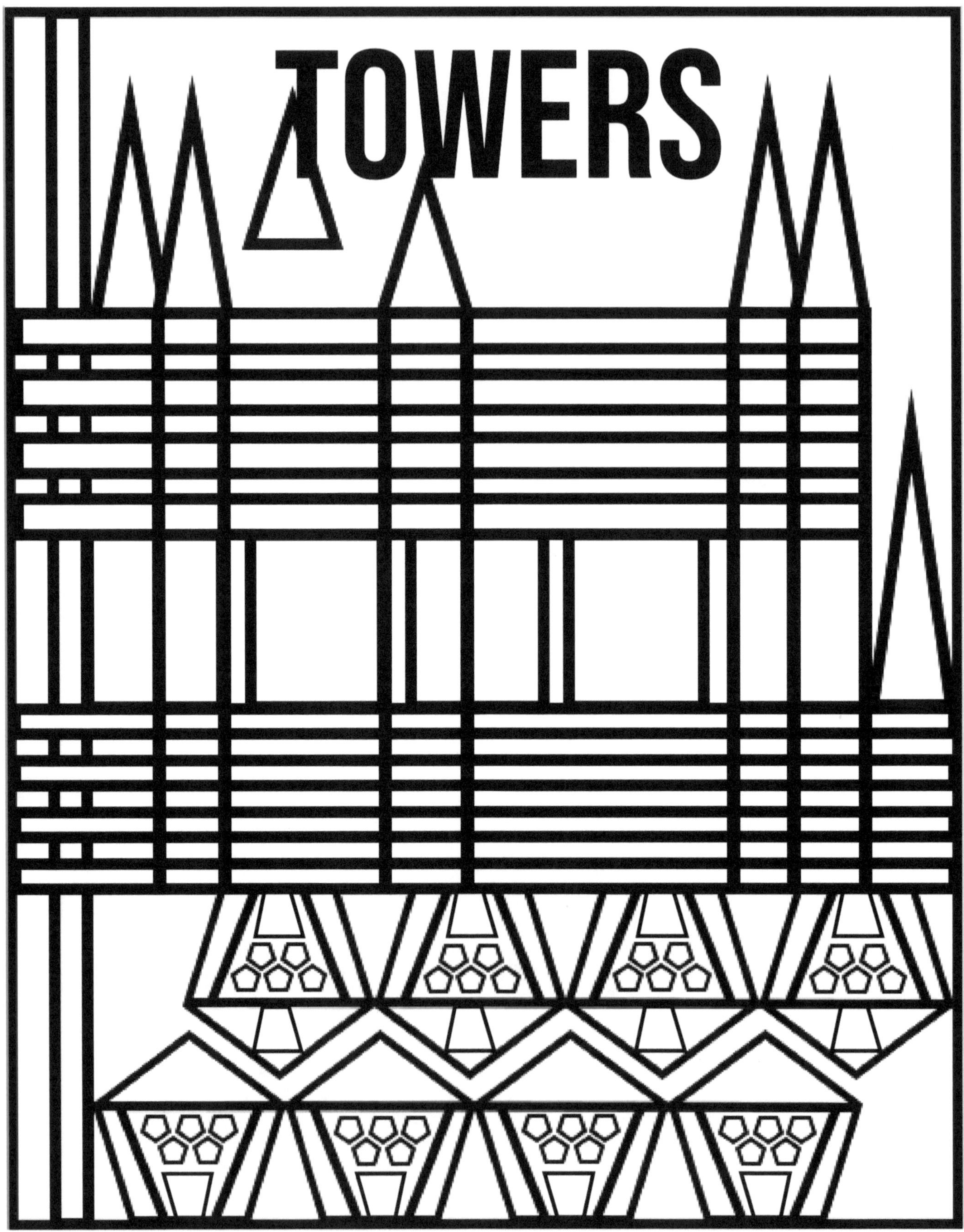

TOWERS

TOWERS

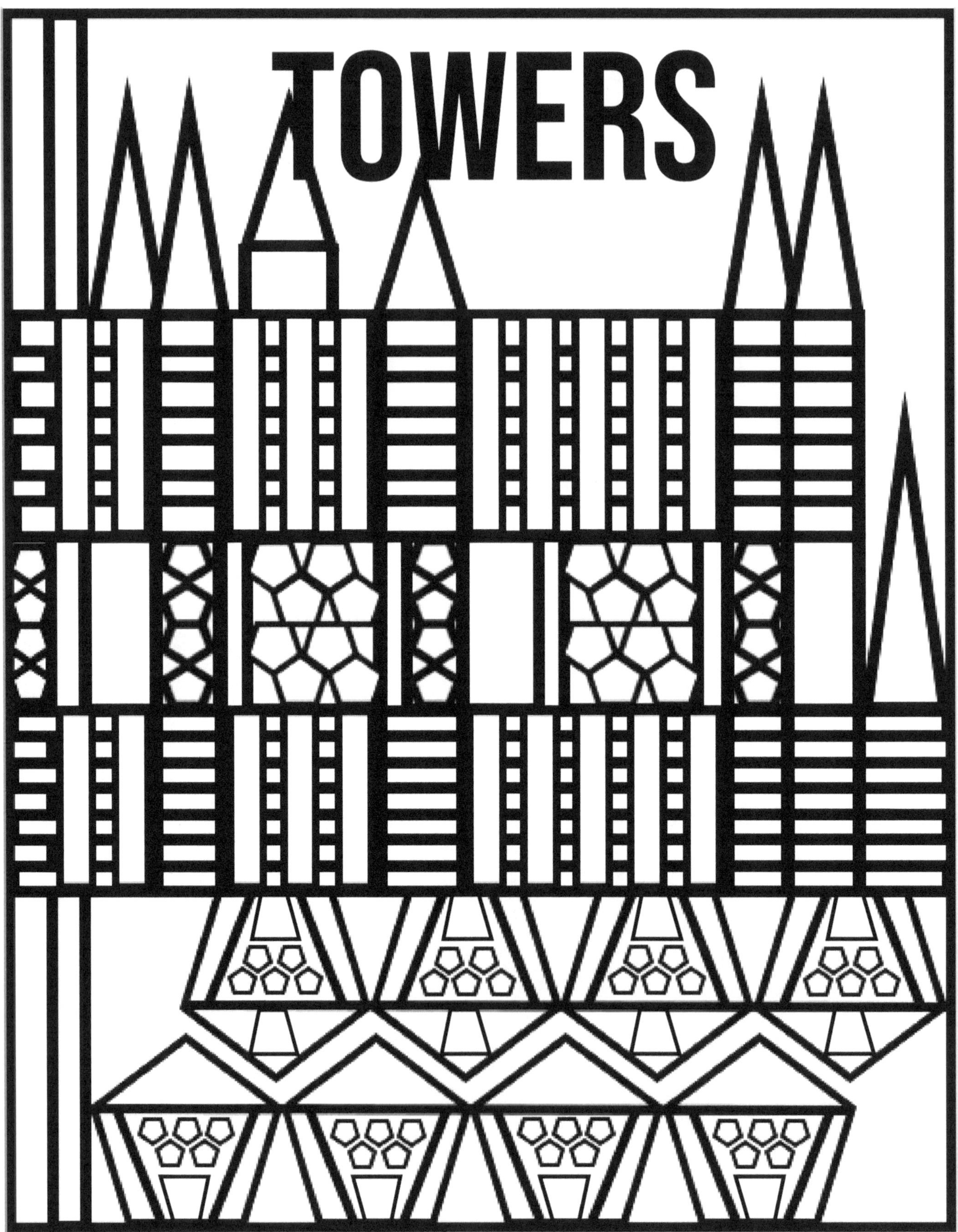

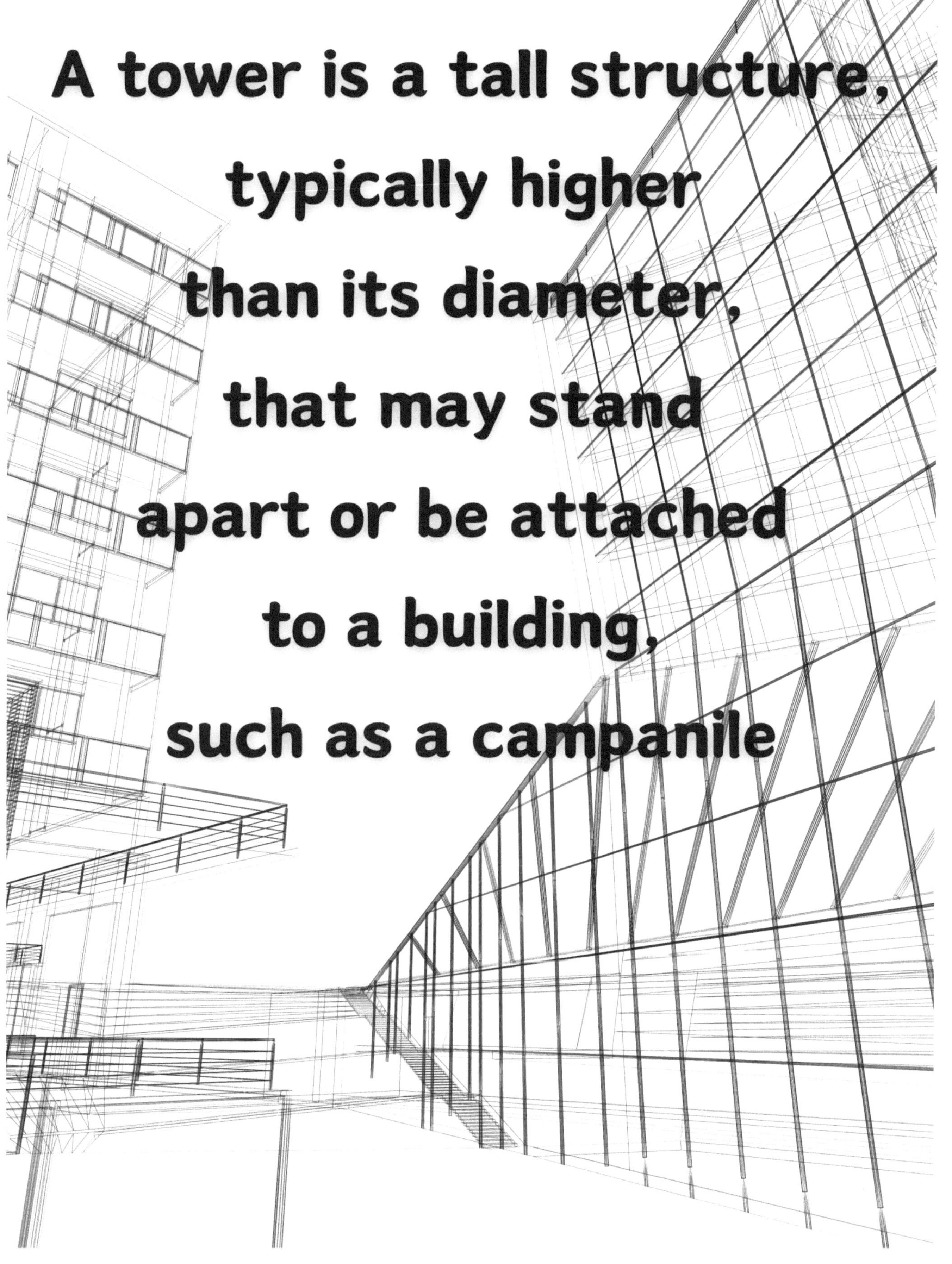

A tower is a tall structure,
typically higher
than its diameter,
that may stand
apart or be attached
to a building,
such as a campanile

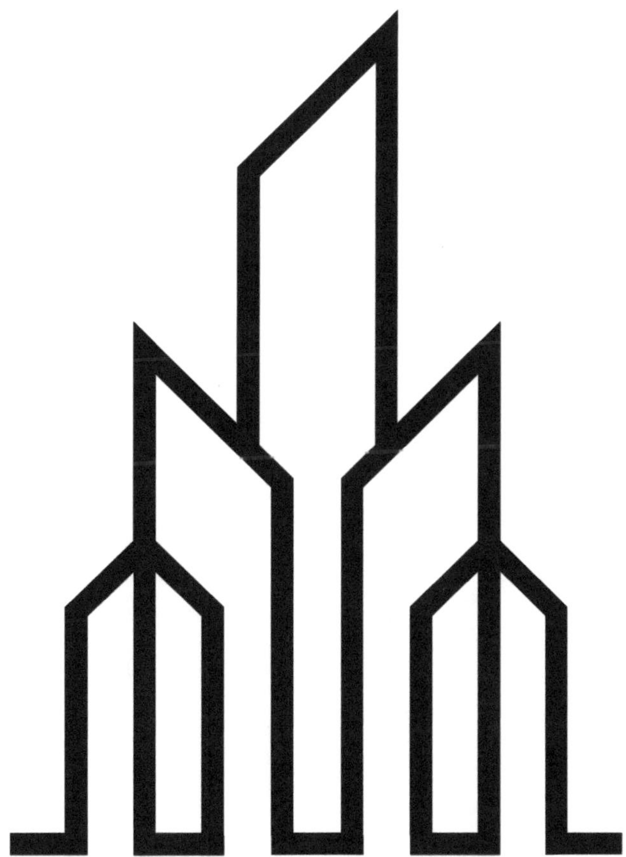

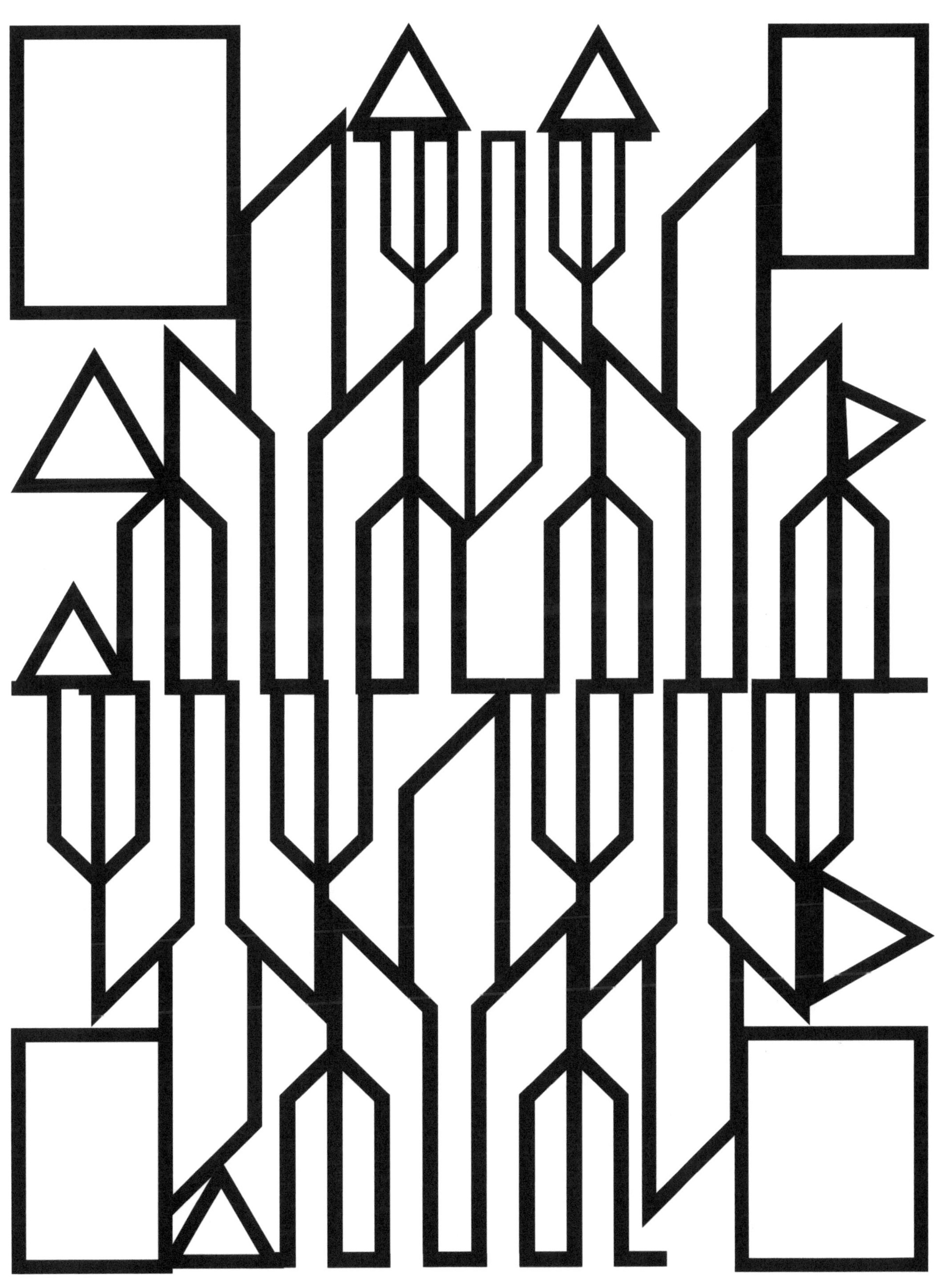

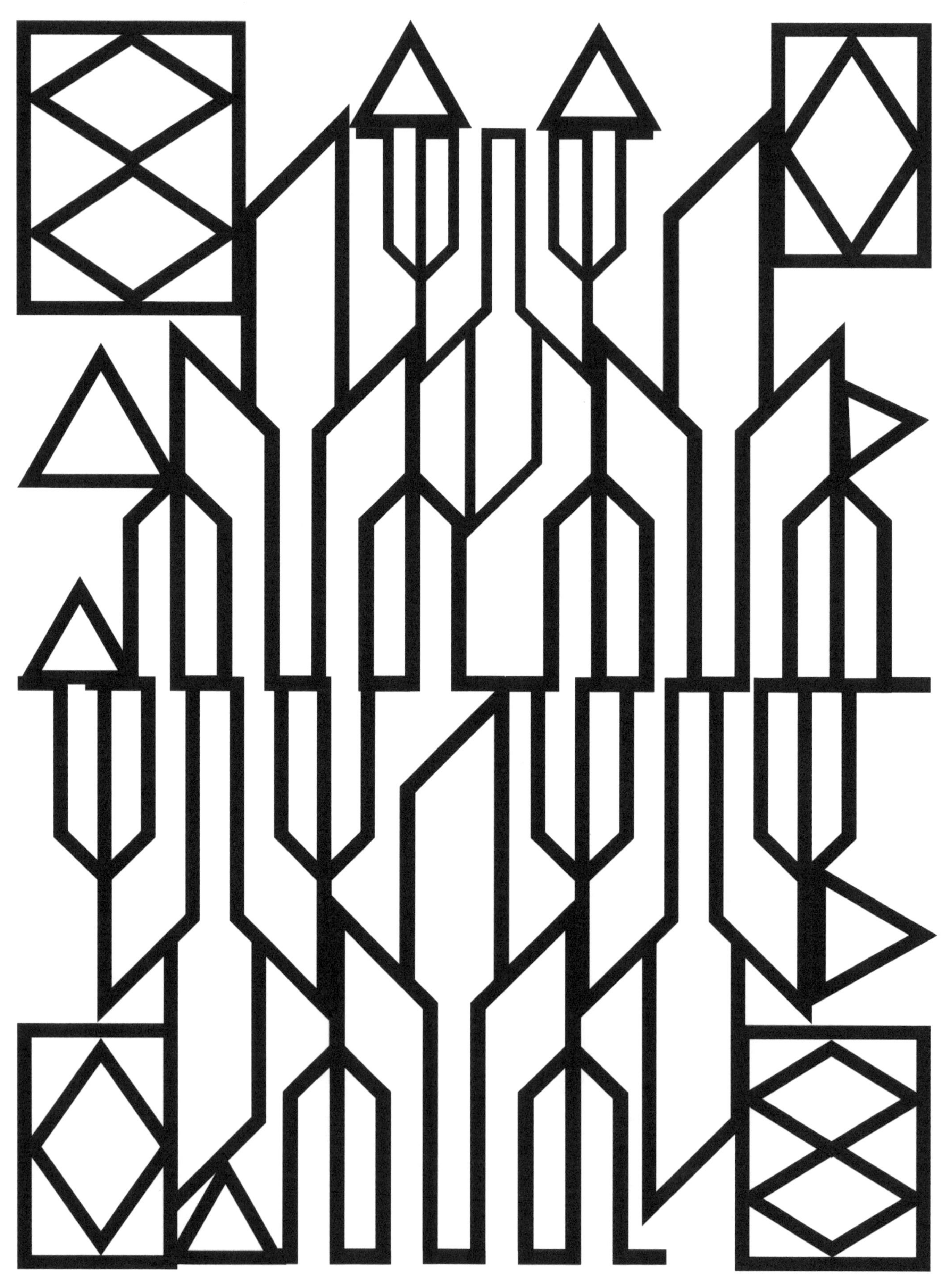

Do sky scrapers really
scrape the sky?
Hmmm...

I hope you enjoyed this phased coloring book. The inspiration for this style is the old timey animation flip books that used to be around before computer animation began. One shape is drawn on the page, them pages later ae a masterpiece has been created.

-Val Singleton

Follow us on Amazon for more
Visit us on social media @sinfulpressure_
www.sinfulpressure.com